A New World

ENGLAND'S FIRST VIEW of AMERICA

WATERCOLORS *by*
JOHN WHITE

Pomegranate

SAN FRANCISCO

Pomegranate Communications, Inc.
Box 808022, Petaluma CA 94975
800 227 1428; www.pomegranate.com

Pomegranate Europe Ltd.
Unit 1, Heathcote Business Centre, Hurlbutt Road
Warwick, Warwickshire CV34 6TD, UK
[+44] 0 1926 430111; sales@pomeurope.co.uk

ISBN 978-0-7649-4014-9
Pomegranate Catalog No. AA374

Pomegranate publishes books of postcards on a wide range of subjects.
Please contact the publisher for more information.

Cover designed by Mariah Lander
Printed in Korea
16 15 14 13 12 11 10 09 08 07   10 9 8 7 6 5 4 3 2 1

To facilitate detachment of the postcards from this book, fold each card along its perforation line before tearing.

THE FIRST WHITE VISITORS described Roanoke Island's inhabitants as "gentle, loving, and faithfull." The next group, some of whom learned the rudiments of the Algonquian language, saw a society so agreeable and submissive that "if we govern them well, they will in a short time become civilized and embrace the true religion." But the writer of these words, Thomas Harriot, also reported a quite different vision of the future, that described by the natives: "They prophesied that more of our generation would yet come to this country to kill them and to take away their homes."

The British surveyor and illustrator John White arrived in Roanoke with Harriot in July 1585, as part of a military colonizing expedition sent by Sir Walter Raleigh to what is now North Carolina. He spent his days sketching the people of the place, his watercolor images enriched by what he learned from Harriot about local mores and culture. The delicate balance of those early days was swiftly upset when the expedition's admiral, Sir Richard Grenville, responded to the alleged theft of a silver cup by torching an empty Algonquian village. After enduring a hard winter, and having alienated the once-friendly inhabitants, the Roanoke colonists fled back to England. Though White courageously returned to Roanoke as governor of a new colony, bringing with him one hundred and fifty men and women (including his pregnant daughter), within a few years virtually the entire colony vanished. One man survived: John White. Away in England to secure much needed provisions, he returned to confront America's most perplexing and enduring mystery.

In making the first ethnographic drawings of Native Americans, White relied on a set of visual tropes visible in his earlier depictions of Inuit, Picts, and Turks: they derive from classical poses and gestures transmitted via Dutch and Italian art. The thirty reproductions of White's watercolors that illustrate this book of postcards convey the struggle to see clearly in a land where all seemed strange and new.

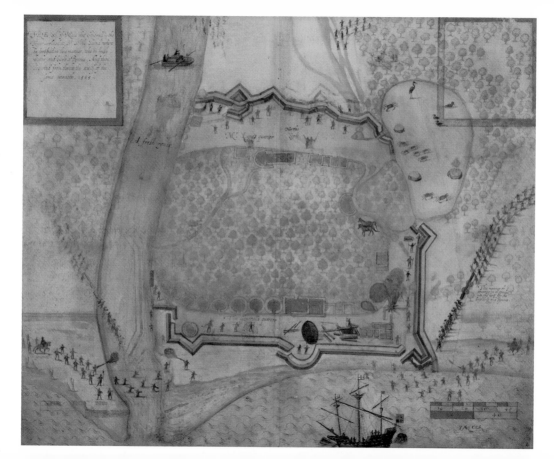

A New World

"THE xjth of Maie the Generall in the Tyger arriued at St Iohns Iland where he fortified in this manner, toke in fresh water, and buylt a Pynnes, And then departed from thence the xxiijth of the same moneth. 1585." Plan of a fortified encampment at Mosquetal (Tallaboa Bay), Puerto Rico. Pen and brown ink over black lead and watercolor, on two conjoined sheets, 36.3 x 44.5 cm. 1906,0509.1.4

The ship on which John White arrived in the New World was obliged to stop in Puerto Rico to build a pinnace, the smaller boat used to ferry people between ship and shore. Visible in the painting are horses recently captured from the Spanish.

BOX 808022   PETALUMA   CA 94975

Pomegranate

Theire sitting at meate.

A New World

"Theire sitting at meate." A Native American man and woman eating. Watercolor and body color over black lead, touched with white, 20.9 x 21.4 cm. 1906,0509.1.20

Until quite recently, the phrase "sit at meat" was used to mean, quite simply, eat. The meal in front of this couple probably consisted of hulled and boiled corn, the sort of food someone of fairly low standing—note the woman's lack of tattoos or ornate beads—might eat every day.

BOX 808022   PETALUMA   CA 94975

Pomegranate

The towne of Pomeiock and true forme of their howses, couered
and enclosed some wth matts, and some wth barcks of trees. All compassed
abowt wth smale poles stock thick together in stedd of a wall.

3

A New World

"The towne of Pomeiock and true forme of their howses, couered and enclosed some wth matts, and some wth barcks of trees. All compassed abowt wth smale poles stock thick together in stedd of a wall." The village of Pomeiooc. Watercolor and body color over black lead, touched with gold, 22.2 x 21.5 cm. 1906,0509.1.8

Longhouses typically were built by tribes living further north: none are known to have occurred south of Roanoke. The painting also shows that Native Americans kept dogs well before Europeans introduced their favorite breeds.

CA 94975

PETALUMA

BOX 808022

A New World

A Pict warrior, male. Pen and brown ink, and watercolor and body color, over black lead, touched with white (oxidized), 24.2 x 15.2 cm. 1906,0509.1.26

In Theodor de Bry's appendix to his illustrated edition of Thomas Harriot's *Briefe and True Report of the New Found Land of Virginia* (1590), he explained that he had included pictures of ancient Scottish figures by John White "to showe how that the Inhabitants of the great Bretannie haue bin in times past as sauuage as those of Virginia." Sir Walter Raleigh had bestowed the name Virginia on what is now North Carolina and South Carolina.

CA 94975

PETALUMA

BOX 808022

Pomegranate

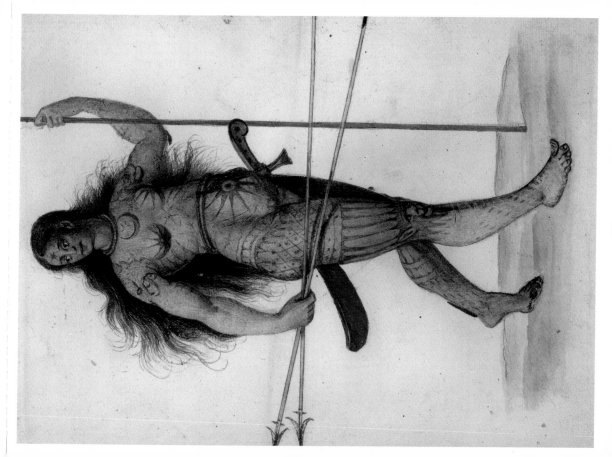

A New World

A Pict warrior, female. Watercolor over black lead, touched with body color, white (oxidized), and pen and ink, 23 x 17.9 cm. 1906,0509.1.27

Some suspect that the contemporaneous conflicts between Protestant English and Catholic Irish informed the fascination with Picts and other ancient savages of the British Isles. Theodor de Bry wrote that Pict woman warriors "wear noe worser for the warres than the men."

BOX 808022   PETALUMA   CA 94975

Pomegranate

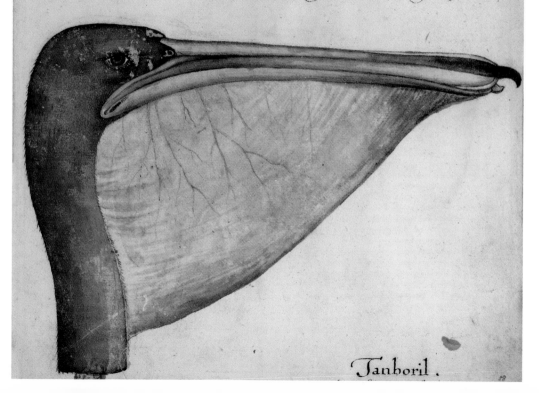

Alcatralsa. This fowle is of the greatnes of a Swanne. and of the same forme sauing the heade, wch is in length .16. ynches.

Tanboril.

A New World

"Alcatrafsa. This fowle is of the greatness of a Swanne and of the same forme sauing the heade, wch is in length 16 ynches." Eastern brown pelican *(Pelecanus occidentalis carolinensis).* Watercolor over black lead, touched with white (?), 18.5 x 22.3 cm. 1906,0509.1.58

Brown pelicans typically nest on small offshore islands, and it is quite possible that Roanoke was home to a breeding colony at the time White was there. (Colonies have been found on nearby islands during the last decade.)

BOX 808022   PETALUMA   CA 94975

Pomegranate

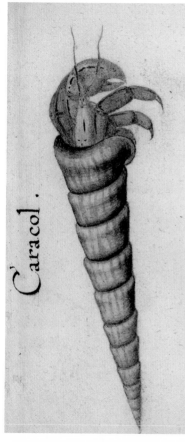

Caracol.

Caracol.

Thes lyue on land neere the Sea lyde, and breede in sondry Shells when they be empty.

1

A New World

"Thes lyue on land neere the Sea syde, and breede in sondry shells when they be empty." Purple-clawed hermit crabs *(Coenobita clypeatus)*. Watercolor and body color over black lead, touched with white, 18.8 x 15.5 cm. 1906,0509.1.57

The hermit crabs painted by White occur in the West Indies; their range does not extend to Roanoke. The original owners of the shells were a variegate screw shell *(Turritella variegata)* and a gaudy natica *(Natica canariensis)*.

BOX 808022   PETALUMA   CA 94975

The manner of their fishing.

A New World

"The manner of their fishing." Indians fishing. Watercolor and body color touched with gold, 35.3 x 23.5 cm. 1906,0509.1.6

Rather than view this fishing scene as a realistic depiction of the numbers and variety of marine animals found near Roanoke, it should be understood as a catalogue of species and the techniques used to take them. Native Americans taught English colonists several of these techniques and even built weirs for them.

Their rype corne.

Their greene corne.

Corne newly sprong.

Their sitting at meate.

SECOTON.

The house wherein the Tombe of their Herowns standeth.

A Ceremony in their prayers wth straing gestures and song dansing abowt posts carved on the topps lyke mens faces.

A New World

"Secoton." The village of Secotan. Watercolor and body color over black lead, heightened with white (oxidized), 32.4 x 19.9 cm. 1906,0509.1.7

The Native American village of Secotan was built on the west side of a large lake identified by White as "Paquippe" and now called Mattamuskeet. Much of the land near the houses was given over to corn, planted on a staggered schedule so as to yield a steady supply. The Secotan people moved several times over the course of the year and did not always return to the same settlements.

BOX 808022   PETALUMA   CA 94975

A land Tort wth the Sauages esteeme aboue all other Torts

A New World

"A land Tort wch the Sauages esteeme aboue all other Torts." Common box turtle *(Terrapene carolina carolina)*. Watercolor over black lead, touched with white (oxidized?), 14.4 x 19.7 cm. 1906,0509.1.68

A totem animal, the box turtle was also eaten and exploited for its medicinal properties by Native Americans. One wonders whether the flesh varies in flavor (and medical efficacy) with age: young box turtles are primarily carnivorous, their elders primarily herbivorous.

BOX 808022   PETALUMA   CA 94975

Pomegranate

A NEW WORLD

A "warrior neighbour of the Picts." Pen and brown ink and watercolor over black lead, touched with white, 23.6 x 15.4 cm. 1906,0509.1.28

In *De bello gallico,* Julius Caesar wrote, "All the Britons, in fact, dye themselves with woad, which imparts a bluish color and makes them more horrifying in battle." Many of the figures painted by White have painted or tattooed their bodies.

BOX 808022   PETALUMA   CA 94975

Pomegranate

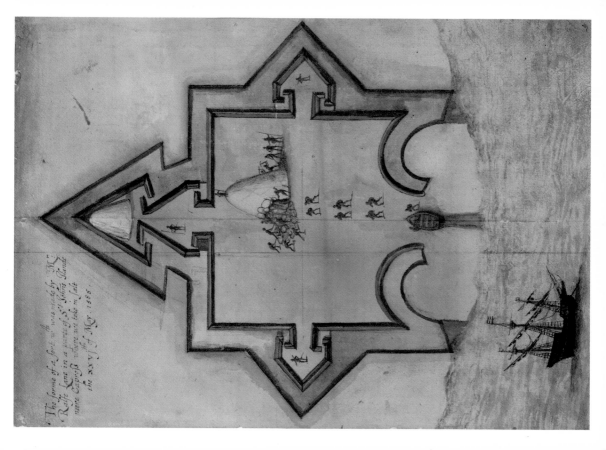

The forme of a fort wch was made by Mr
Rallf Lane in a prymry of St Johns Iland
were Caprges where we toke in Salt
the xxv of May 1585.

A New World

"The forme of a fort wch was made by M: Ralfe Lane in a parte of St Iohns Ilande neere Capross where we toke in salt the xxvjth of May. 1585." Plan of an entrenchment near Cape Rojo, Puerto Rico. Pen and brown ink over black lead, with watercolor and white body color, 31.5 x 22 cm. 1906,0509.1.5

In a daring move, the captain of the *Tyger* decided to excavate badly needed salt on an island under close observation by Spanish forces. The painting shows a captured Spanish frigate and, on shore, men digging out the salt with pickaxes while others stand guard.

BOX 808022   PETALUMA   CA 94975

Pomegranate

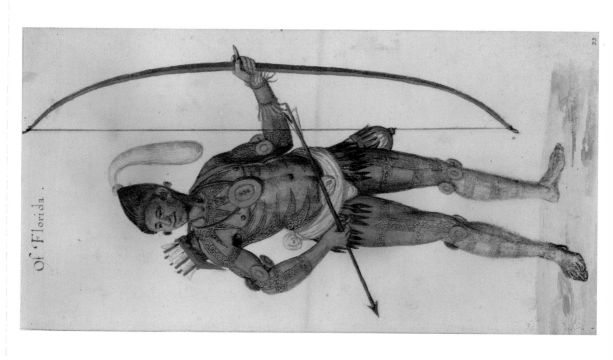

Of Florida.

A New World

"Of Florida." A Timucua man. John White (after Jacques Le Moyne de Morgues). Pen and brown ink and watercolor over black lead, with body color touched with silver (?) (oxidized), gold, and white (oxidized), 26.8 x 13.7 cm. 1906,0509.1.22

This painting was almost certainly a copy White made from the work of Jacques Le Moyne de Morgues (French, c. 1533–1588), who visited Florida in 1564. Le Moyne's originals have been lost, but a number of copies by other artists have survived.

BOX 808022   PETALUMA   CA 94975

Pomegranate

42

A NEW WORLD

"Oio de buey." Squirrelfish *(Holocentrus adscensionis).* Watercolor over black lead, touched with white (oxidized) and gold, 13.2 x 19.9 cm. 1906,0509.1.42

The principal motive for the voyages to America directed by Sir Walter Raleigh was financial. He instructed White and the expedition's scientist, Thomas Harriot (an early champion of the medicinal properties of tobacco), to focus on exploitable commodities: this fish, found in the West Indies and along the Atlantic coast of America, is edible.

BOX 808022   PETALUMA   CA 94975

Pomegranate

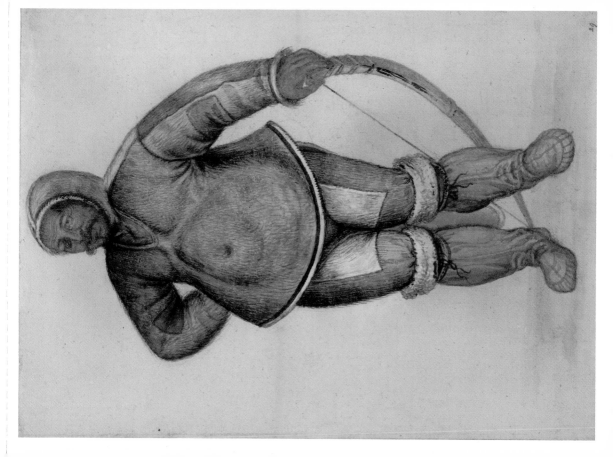

A New World

"Kalicho," an Inuk from Frobisher Bay. Pen and brown ink and watercolor over black lead, touched with white (oxidized), 22.7 x 16.4 cm. 1906,0509.1.29

This man was taken captive near Baffin Island on what was then called Hall's Greater Island and is now called Loks Land in English and Takuligjuaq in Inuktitut. White painted him in England, where he was taken by English sailors led by Martin Frobisher, an explorer seeking the arctic boundary between Europe, Greenland, America, and Asia. He died less than four months after his capture.

BOX 808022   PETALUMA   CA 94975

Pomegranate

The Pyne frute.

41

A New World

"The Pyne frute." Pineapple *(Ananas comosus)*. Watercolor over black lead, touched with white, 25.8 x 14.1 cm. 1906,0509.1.41

Sir Walter Raleigh named it "the princess of fruits." European explorers had seen to it that the pineapple, which originated in Brazil and Paraguay, was planted in many of the world's tropical areas by the time White arrived in Puerto Rico in 1585.

BOX 808022   PETALUMA   CA 94975

Pomegranate

Garopa.

48

A New World

"Garopa." Grouper or rock hind *(Epinephelus adscensionis).*
Watercolor over black lead, touched with gold and silver (or white)
(oxidized), 9.3 x 21.8 cm. 1906,0509.1.48

The identity of this fish is doubtful. Though White labeled it "Garopa,"
the Spanish word for grouper, modern illustrations of *Epinephelus
adscensionis* differ from this one in several ways.

BOX 808022   PETALUMA   CA 94975

Pomegranate

A cheife Herowans wyfe of Pomeoc. and her daughter of the age of .8. or. .10. yeares.

A New World

"A cheife Herowans wyfe of Pomeoc and her daughter of the age of 8 or 10 yeares." A Native American woman and child of Pomeiooc. Watercolor and body color over black lead, touched with white, 26.3 x 14.9 cm. 1906,0509.1.13

A native girl shows her mother a fancy doll given her by the colonists. Sir Walter Raleigh, the instigator and backer of the Roanoke expeditions, promised that these ventures would open huge new markets for British trade.

BOX 808022   PETALUMA   CA 94975

Pomegranate

the Roller.

A New World

European roller *(Coracias garrulus).* Pen and watercolor over black lead, with body color, touched with white, 16 x 22.6 cm. 1906,0509.1.64

Not a New World species (as one would guess from the name), the roller occurs now largely in Turkey, Greece, and Spain. It perches on a tree or a post, awaiting the appearance of a scorpion, centipede, lizard, or frog—then dives.

BOX 808022   PETALUMA   CA 94975

Pomegranate

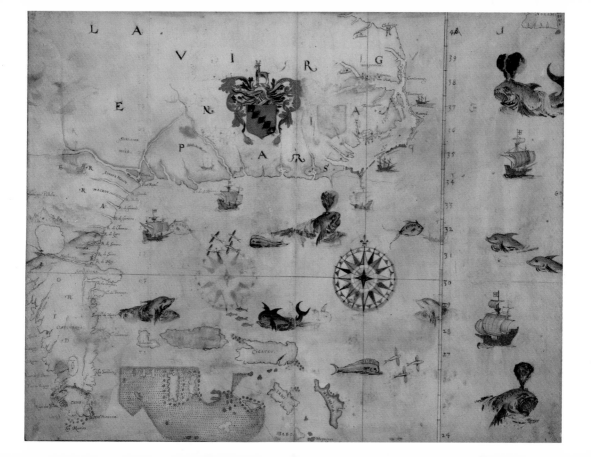

A New World

"La Virgenia Pars." Map of the east coast of North America from
Chesapeake Bay to the Florida Keys. Pen and brown ink over black
lead, with watercolor, touched with white (oxidized) and gold,
37 x 47.2 cm. 1906,0509.1.2

As if claiming the territory of Virginia (what is now North Carolina
and South Carolina), the coat of arms of Sir Walter Raleigh is spread
over the land in the upper part of the map at left.

CA 94975

PETALUMA

BOX 808022

Pomegranate

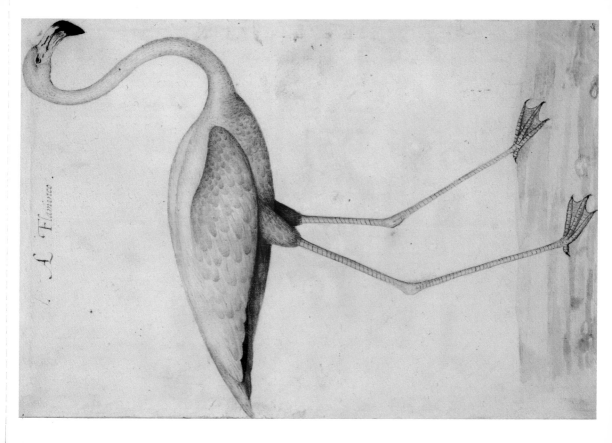

A Flamingo.

A New World

"A Flaminco." Greater flamingo *(Phoenicopterus ruber).* Watercolor over black lead, touched with white (oxidized), 29.6 x 19.7 cm. 1906,0509.1.60

White must have seen flamingoes while passing through the Bahamas or the West Indies, as they rarely occur in North America. Only after this expedition did other travelers discover that this animal is edible.

BOX 808022 PETALUMA CA 94975

Pomegranate

Of Florida.

A New World

"Of Florida." A Timucua woman. John White (after Le Moyne).
Pen and brown ink and watercolor over black lead, with body-
color, touched with gold and silver (?) (oxidized), 26.1 x 13.5 cm.
1906,0509.1.23

Probably a copy White made from the work of Jacques Le Moyne de
Morgues (French, c. 1533–1588), this painting depicts a native of
northeast Florida whose livelihood depended on farming corn, squash,
and beans. A dedicated follower of fashion, she wears inflated fish
bladders in her ears.

BOX 808022   PETALUMA   CA 94975

Pomegranate

A New World

Magnificent frigate bird *(Fregata magnificens)*. Watercolor over black lead, touched with white, 13.6 x 22.3 cm. 1906,0509.1.62

Their plumage easily soaked, their feet too small for walking, frigate birds exist as pure creatures of the atmosphere. They feed on squid and flying fish at or near the ocean's surface without ever wetting a feather and also obtain food by acts of piracy practiced on other birds.

BOX 808022   PETALUMA   CA 94975

Pomegranate

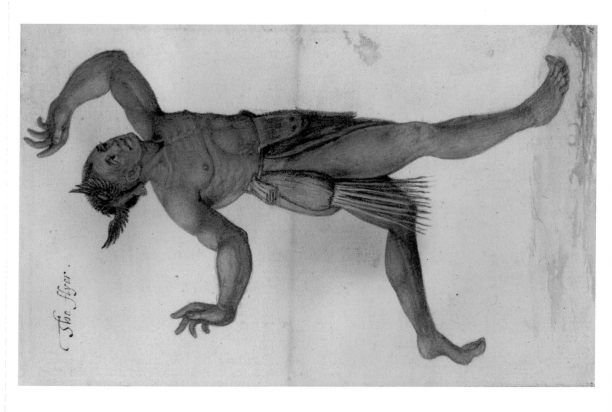

The flyer.

A NEW WORLD

"The flyer." A Native American medicine man. Watercolor over black lead, touched with white (oxidized), 24.6 x 15.1 cm. 1906,0509.1.16

Is this a pose that John White seized while watching the dance of an Algonquian medicine man, or has he imposed the traditional posture of Hermes (messenger of the gods) on a subject quite alien to Western traditions?

BOX 808022   PETALUMA   CA 94975

Pomegranate

A lande Crab.

A New World

"A lande Crab." Blue land crab *(Cardisoma guanhumi).* Watercolor
and body color over black lead, touched with white (oxidized),
23.3 x 27.6 cm. 1906,0509.1.56

Probably painted in the West Indies, this crab is a terrestrial burrow-
dweller found in mangrove swamps and along beaches. In addition to
leaves and fruit, the blue land crab eats insects, feces, and carrion.

BOX 808022   PETALUMA   CA 94975

Pomegranate

A New World

A Turk, with a scimitar. Watercolor over black lead, with some white body color, 22.6 x 15.6 cm. 1906,0509.1.31

A sixteenth-century bogeyman, the Turk threatened virtuous Christians on the Elizabethan stage even as he filled the coffers of British merchants with gold. The model for this image is unknown.

A New World

Common hoopoe *(Upopa epops).* Pen and brown ink and watercolor over black lead, heightened with white (oxidized), 15 x 21.1 cm. 1906,0509.1.61

Once believed to possess magical powers, including the ability to predict the weather, the hoopoe is a bird that sounds like a dog, looks like a giant butterfly, and, when threatened, assumes a posture that makes it look "like an old parti-colored rag," according to the nineteenth-century authority J. E. Harting, F.L.S., F.Z.S.

BOX 808022   PETALUMA   CA 94975

Pomegranate

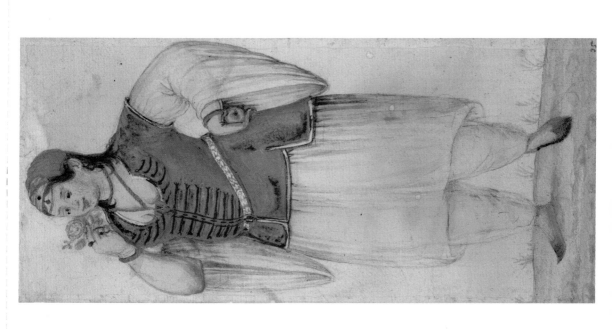

A New World

A Greek or Turkish woman, with a rose and a pomegranate.
Watercolor over black lead, touched with white body color and
silver (?) (oxidized), 21 x 9.4 cm. 1906,0509.1.35

In addition to the luxury goods being exported from Turkey during
John White's lifetime, there was quite a trade in Turkish tales and
orientalist images. The pomegranate was closely associated with
femininity, thanks to its shape and a flavor said to have enticed both
Eve and Adam.

BOX 808022   PETALUMA   CA 94975

Pomegranate

A New World

Atlantic loggerhead turtle *(Caretta caretta caretta)*. Watercolor and body color over black lead, touched with white, 18.7 x 26 cm. 1906,0509.1.70

Thomas Harriot, who accompanied White on the first expedition to Roanoke, wrote of the local sea turtles: "Their heads, feet, and tails look very ugly, like those of a venomous serpent. Nevertheless, they are very good to eat, as are their eggs." He probably did not have the loggerhead in mind, since most have found its flesh quite vile.

BOX 808022   PETALUMA   CA 94975

Pomegranate

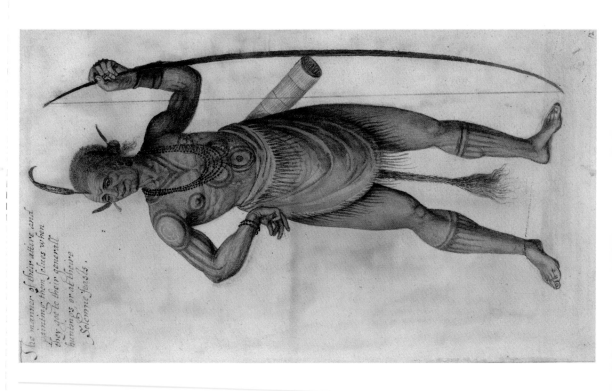

The manner of their attire and
painting them selues when
they goe to their generall
huntings or att theire
Solemne feasts.

A New World

"The manner of their attire and painting them selues when they goe to their generall huntings, or at theire Solemne feasts." An Algonquian man painted for a great solemn gathering. Watercolor and body color over black lead, touched with white, 26.3 x 15 cm. 1906,0509.1.12

The pose of this figure—possibly a chief, to judge from his ornaments—is classical: White unconsciously borrowed from the vocabulary of European figure painting to endow his subject with authority.

BOX 808022 PETALUMA CA 94975

Pomegranate